F IS FOR FRENCH QUARTER

By Scott & Tallulah Campbell

Illustrated by Nichole Dupre

PELICAN PUBLISHING
New Orleans 2022

ISBN 9781455626717
E-book ISBN 9781455626724

Printed in Korea

Published by Pelican Publishing
New Orleans, LA
www.pelicanpub.com

Behold the many wonders of the French Quarter.

To my kids. Do what's hard and life will be easy.—SC
I dedicate this book to my sister, Delilah.—TC

A is for Audubon Aquarium of the Americas. It's in the French Quarter!

artist   Aunt Sally's Pralines

C is for Café Du Monde.
It's in the French Quarter!

E is for Esplanade Avenue. It's in the French Quarter!

Easter parades

Easter Bunny

F is for French Quarter.

festival

football fans

FRENCH MARKET

families

fortune teller

FRENCH QUARTER

H is for haunted history.
It's in the French Quarter!

humidity

historic homes

I is for Iberville Street.
It's in the French Quarter!

Mardi Gras Indian

K is for Krewe du Vieux. It's in the French Quarter!

kids

Mardi Gras

king cake

N is for Napoleon House.
It's in the French Quarter!

narcissus

Q is for Queens of New Orleans.
They love the French Quarter!

R is for Roman candy. It's in the French Quarter!

The French Quarter is an eXcellent place to visit!

Washington Artillery Park

eXcellent place to Visit!

waterfront

Zip around and get to know the French Quarter.